Looking for Patterns

by Margie Burton, Cathy French, and Tammy Jones

Patterns are things that repeat in the same way.

Some patterns are big.

Some patterns are small.

Sometimes things have patterns.

Sometimes you make patterns.

3

You can find patterns everywhere.
You can find patterns on a bed,

on
the walls,

and on the floor.

You can find patterns when you get dressed.

The clothes have a striped pattern.

You can find patterns when you eat.

You can find patterns when you
play games inside with your friends.

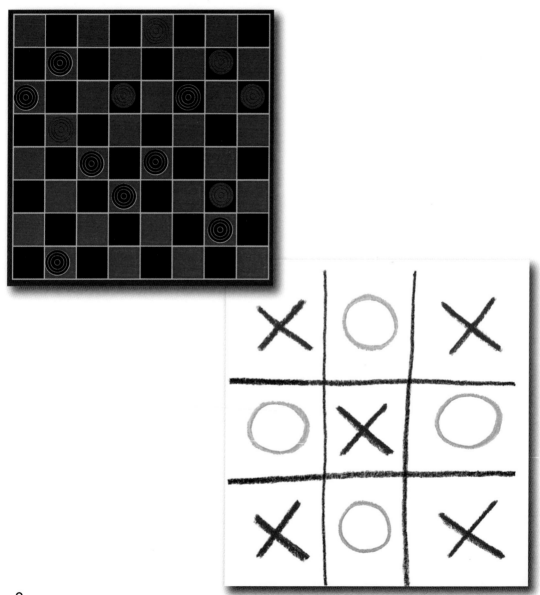

You can find patterns when
you play outside with your friends.

You can find patterns when you
take a walk in the fields,

or at the beach.

Some patterns can help us
by telling us things.

You can tell how old a tree was
by looking at the rings on the trunk
after the tree has been cut down.

Each ring stands for one year's growth. A ring
is made up of both a light part and a dark part.

Patterns help us when we play the piano.

Patterns help us know what time it is.

Patterns can help keep you safe.

This pattern helps us know where it is safe to cross the street.

Our world is made up of many patterns.